The Reality Creator's Handbook

Copyright © 2014 by Mark Allen Frost

First Edition

Seth Returns Publishing

Editorial: Mark Frost

Cover Design, Typography & Layout:

Mark Frost

Cover Photo Courtesy Goddess of Love

Library of Congress Control Number: 2014918755

ISBN 13: 9780982694640

ISBN 10: 0-9826946-4-4

CONTENTS

Introduction by Mark..............................v

Introduction by Seth............................vii

Forward - The Moon and Natural Time......ix

1 - Waking Up Now................................ 1

2 - The Best Case Scenario.........................15

Illustration - BCS Flow Chart.....................19

3 - The Telepathic Network.......................33

4 - Picking Up the Trail............................43

5 - Getting Lost...................................59

6 - Fulfillment....................................67

7 - Returning.....................................75

Epilogue...81

Ritual of Sanctuary................................83

Glossary...85

When You Walk Across the Room............95

Introduction by Mark

Welcome to *The Reality Creator's Handbook*. This book was created specifically for you to be used as a guidebook for creating your personal realities and for your awakenings. The Reality Creator's Project lasts for about 28 days, roughly the lunar cycle. Each day or phase of the moon is a Lesson. Each week or each Chapter is a leg of the Journey. You are setting yourself up for an awakening at the end of four weeks, as you read the text and do the exercises.

Seth teaches that each of us has Issues, and as we learn our Lessons by transforming those liabilities into assets, we awaken to our individual enlightened realities. We become awake in the **New Consciousness** of the Fourth Dimension and beyond.

I learned a lot about the Seth teaching when I was in India in May of this year. Seth told me before I left for the trip that I would be transformed when I returned to the states. He was right, as usual. But he didn't tell me that the transformation would continue and intensify. I am in the middle of it now. For the most part, it has to do with finding a way to re-create the higher consciousness I experienced in the Himalayas, here in my mundane reality. I will have more to say about it on the website and possibly in ***Seth on Death and the Afterlife***

Have fun with the new book! Remember, sometimes our Lessons are all about how to learn to have fun and enjoy ourselves in the physical dimension.

Introduction by Seth

Greetings, Dear Reader. This latest effort is a condensed version of my Teaching. However, make no mistake, these pages contain the vital essence of the Ancient Wisdom, the source of all of my material that I have created with my collaborators. Nothing of importance has been left out, yet much is implied in the words in this new volume. By "implied," I mean **subtext**, and by subtext, I mean my particular definition for this word. Refer to the glossary for our accepted definition of subtext.

You already know this material. It is imprinted in your DNA, as I have often suggested to you. It is our hope that through reading these efforts at spiritual literature, your consciousness will be catalyzed, indeed, initiated magically into a greater appreciation for your own personal reality.

Originally we were going to title this book *The Co-Creator's Handbook*. We wished at that time to emphasize the necessary connection to Source that empowers these practices. Then we decided to present this simplified version of my Teaching for all students, even the agnostics. For in the end, we are all talking about consciousness by way of metaphors of various types. We should not direct these messages toward a group that favors one metaphor over another. All metaphors are welcome here. Please note, Mark, that I am attempting humor at this time.

Mark: OK Seth.

This material I am providing to you as a service to humanity. I am attempting to bring you further along on the evolutionary trail, so that you may be comfortable functioning in the New Consciousness.

Please notice that I begin each Chapter with a segment I call One of My Students. This I do to give you a flavor of what is to come in the book. I believe this helps to draw you into these messages.

Additionally, first references of important concepts are printed in bold, so that you may turn to the Glossary for more information on the subject matter.

And as usual, please create **Sanctuary** for yourself before you conduct the exercises. We have provided the Ritual of Sanctuary at the back of the book.

Then we shall begin...

The Moon and Natural Time

Let me state the obvious, just for a moment... The sun rises and sets in the daytime sky. The moon rises and sets in the nighttime sky. From horizon to horizon you can easily see with your own eyes, these phenomena of light marking the passage of time. The sun as it lights your daytime may be a personal matter for you. You come to know this star, then, and you rely on it for its constancy. It is a very loyal friend, is it not, this distant star of yours? It is indeed a friend to Earth and those beings that live upon and within her.

Now the moon has a different quality, if I may say so. The moon is your friend after the sun is gone for the day. There is something that kindles your human emotions in this moon. Indeed, throughout your histories, the poet, the scientist and the average citizen have all agreed that moonlight is a potent catalyst in the emotional life of human beings.

Because most of our readers will be quite able to mark the progression of the moon through its phases, we have chosen this celestial timepiece to help us mark our way through this program of co-creating personal realities. We will suggest particular phases of the moon to appreciate and observe as you implement various aspects of the system I am teaching you in this manuscript. You may use this information or ignore it completely, however. My assistant Mark finds it useful to note the passage of the moon. It assists him in reinitiating his sense of Natural Time within his consciousness.

The suggested meanings of the moon phases that I offer in the following pages, such as Intend, Initiate, and so on, are in fact inducements for you-the-reader to enjoy very positive **Altared States** of consciousness. They are my own interpretations, however, and if you would like to create your own personalized meanings of the phases of the moon, please do so. These suggestions, as with all of our suggestions in our new books, you may take, leave or edit to suit your individual awakening consciousness.

Your experience begins with the Balsamic Moon. This is that phase of the moon in which plans are made.

Days 1-4
Balsamic Moon
Intend

Chapter 1
Waking Up Now

*"If you are awakening there is no mistaking it.
You are changing. You are becoming
wise and strong."*

One of my Students: During one of our workshops, a man approached the bookstore owner and asked to be allowed into our group for free as he had no money, and was "called by spirit" to attend. Mark took a break from the group and met the man in the lobby. Though Mark was at first reluctant to provide a free ticket for the man, he saw a sparkle of recognition in the man's eyes. The man joined the workshop and was quite a remarkable addition, in retrospect. This is how you keep appointments with Soul Family members.

SETH

Hello, Dear Reader. Welcome to my new project, a book designed to assist those of you who are awakening at this time. This book is for the investigator looking into the truth of the matter, with regards to the personal and the public, the intimate and the collective realities **that you create.**

From my perspective, then, you are <u>already</u> a Reality Creator. Now if you are a fan of my new messages to humanity, you know MY feelings on the subject. The question is, what are YOUR feelings on this idea that you are the creator of your world?

Do you 'buy into' this concept?

Your **beliefs** are the foundation of your created realities. You literally send your creative energies through your beliefs, to imprint your personal realities upon the world.

Are you comfortable with being your own authority?

The path to awakening and the New Consciousness of **Instant Manifestation** leads you away from authorities of all types. You begin to enjoy the freedom of living an unobstructed life.

Do you feel a twinge of shame triggered by your religious conditioning?

This is quite normal. You are challenging generations of religious dogma. Naturally there may be some fear that comes up and some shame that makes itself known. My advice is to move Courageously forward, despite these **Negative Emotions**. This becomes easier to do the more that you do it.

And most importantly, are you beginning to see how much of your world is created subconsciously by you without much conscious input?

This **subconscious projection** accounts for many of the Negative Realities you may be experiencing. Do you feel that you might like to correct that situation, by gaining some conscious control over your Reality Creation efforts? Then you are in the right place for that endeavor. This book will show you how to begin to "consciously" create your physical body and EVERYTHING ELSE that you see in your world, and awaken to the Truth of your system.

For again, as you may already know, we are asserting that you literally create yourself and your world out of your own consciousness. Your body and your world are the projections of your personal and greater consciousness made manifest in the physical world.

Higher Centers of Awareness

Please allow me to continue to present more background information for those of you who may be new to this material.

As you go about your business of creating your body and your world, you are also collaborating with your greater consciousness that includes what we call the **non-physical beings**. These Energy Bodies include the Primary Creator Gestalt I refer to as **All That Is**. Also included in this creative enterprise are the inputs from your personal psyche in this timeframe, the communication streams from your other reincarnational existences - past, present and future lives, in other words - and the formative influences of non-physical **Gestalts of Consciousness** known as Energy Personalities, the Ancestors, Helper Spirits, Guides, **gods**, **goddesses**, Angels, and so on. The New Consciousness of awakened humanity that I speak of in my new books, is being created through these conversations with the non-physical beings. And obvious-

Soul Mate and Soul Family

The concepts of **Soul Mate** and **Soul Family** are integral to my theory of reincarnational family interactions. Briefly, you come into physical existence with both a history - memories of your reincarnational lives, which you promptly forget - and an agenda: a broad plan from Soul outlining Issues and Lessons to be considered in the coming life. Nothing is set in stone, however. You have free will to do as you wish. Yet your history of lives sets you up for a particular style of life.

Additionally, you live your lives with the same group of people, lifetime after lifetime. We call this group the Soul Family. Each one of you in this reincarnational family adopts a different role each lifetime, trying on different bodies, of different genders and sexual orientations, talents and perceived deficits, in a type of repertory dramatic presentation for yourself, your Soul Family and for All That Is. The Soul Family includes potential Soul Mates, that we describe as the Lovers who are awakening together. They are identifying their Issues and Learning their Lessons together. Let me talk a bit about this vital concept...

Issues and Lessons

Dear Reader, if you are awakening now there is no mistaking it. You are changing. You are becoming wise and strong. This awakening takes you on a particular journey in which the truth of your personality and the reasons for your stay on Earth at this time become known to you. You become acquainted with your **Issues** and **Lessons** in this way. Your Issues are those aspects of personality that serve to pit you against others and create Negative Emotion. Your Lessons have to do with if and how you identify your Issues, take responsibility for them, and attempt to heal them

For Example: Perhaps you have been identified as "sickly" by your Soul Family, and you took this designation so seriously that you became a sickly child, then a sickly adult. However, now you are awakening and seeing the truth of the matter. You are no longer weak and sickly, you are transforming into a strong and powerful human. You are thinking, feeling, and behaving like a strong and powerful person, and thus, you are becoming one. We would say that you are now learning your Lesson. You have identified your Issue, that of playing the role of sickly person in your family. You are turning it around, by creating the opposite persona or role for yourself. Do you see?

Loving Understanding and Courage

Let me briefly describe the antidote for negativity, the cure-all for all Negative Realities that confront you: Loving Understanding and Courage. **Loving Understanding** is what you do while you are waiting for your Reality Creation project to manifest. It is that simple. And it does take **Courage** with a capital C to move forward in spite of perceived obstacles, and despite the protestations and even sabotaging efforts of others. Your own **Ego/Intellect** will not be comfortable with your awakening to your power as a Reality Creator, at least at first. Others in your world may resist and deny your new awakening consciousness, for they have grown used to the "you" that they know. In terms of **frequency**, I would say that this illustrates the **Resonance** phenomenon. As you increase your frequency, you may create dissonance with others who are not at your current level of Reality Creation.

Good Humor

Good Humor is the starting point for Positive Realities. It is that Altared State of awareness in which you are easily co-existing with all of the influences in your environment. You are engaged in those behaviors that please you. You are soothing your-self, by fulfilling the desires of your body, mind and spirit. Through this focus on your simple desires, comes this state of flow, of integrity, of pleasant acquiescence to the positive in your world. With this in mind, as you begin to think about what your Reality Creation Project might entail, assume a state of Good Humor consciousness, as you understand it. This is an excellent state of consciousness from which to discover what types of changes you wish to make in your life.

Scientists of Consciousness

Before we end this chapter with an Exercise, I must share with you my idea of who you really are, as an explorer of your own psyche. This may prove to be an excellent role that you can explore and embody... You are a **Scientist of Consciousness**, Dear Reader. As you Courageously go forward, identifying your Issues and learning your Lessons, you quite naturally discover the Truth about your identity and about your world. These discoveries take the form of Findings, as you conduct your experiments and document the outcomes in some way. You then assemble the material and examine these Findings at regular intervals during your project, during your life.

Trust but Verify

Now your scientific instruments are your **Inner Senses**, what you might call your Intuition, and your process is one of **Trust but Verify**. As material seems to come to you from your Source, you take it as Truth, but you also attempt to verify it in some way.

For Example: If you receive what appears to be prophetic material, you may verify it by seeing if it holds true in physical reality over the course of time.

Trust but Verify also works in the ordinary assessment of the human in front of you. You speak to their Energy Personality, you see, to THEIR Higher Centers of Awareness, to assess who they truly are, what they represent, and so on. You then accept the information as truthful, but you do indeed verify it with your own Source. As you engage in these etheric communications you do get better at it, you do find that you are learning how to identify Truth within the static, chaos and misperceptions of your world.

Emotion Mapping

The first exercise of the book is a piece I call Emotion Mapping with the Moon. It is quite simple and enjoyable to do this exercise. It may already be familiar to you as a student of your own Reality Creations. By Emotion Mapping, what I am attempting to convey to you is this: If you may think of yourself as a collaborative effort between your aspect of Evolutionary Consciousness and the whole of consciousness - All That - does it not make sense that your emotional make-up and expression at any given time might mirror the moon in its phases? I do not wish to be flippant here, but, "It does if you think it does," Dear Reader. You create your world according to the varying sensory inputs of consciousness that you call beliefs. You are immersed in an intriguing manuscript that is lulling you into a sense of sublime connection to everything that exists. That is my suggestion. Of course it makes sense that you may, in a manner of speaking, "comprehend" your own countenance in the reflection of the moon. It may meet you in a quite literal sense. If you do believe, then go with that sensing. You will receive valuable feedback from this body of light as we roll out our theory in this little book.

Exercise:
Emotion Mapping with the Moon

Create Sanctuary Now

If you are willing to be this true believer, this moon-entranced visionary type, then here is your assignment. Whatever you do in your life, whatever exercises from this book that you attempt or you ignore, please attend to a simple observation of the moon. Note where the moon rests in its particular phase within your nightscape. Note this Dear Reader, and get a sense of how this station of repose is also reflected in your **Emotional Body**. Your Emotional Body is an inner perception of you-the-reader. There in symbolic or even literal form are your Issues and Lessons of physical existence; the reasons you are on Earth currently, in other words.

Please do not over-think this concept. Have fun with it. Look for correlations between the phases of the moon and the changes within your Emotional Body over time. For your moon tugs at this Emotional Body of yours. It pulls you out of shape sometimes, and it pushes you back in at times also. This is what I mean by Emotion Mapping: you are marking the emotional territory within your consciousness that correlates to the light display of the moon. Again, do not over-think this. Entertain these suggestions lightly, as a child would. Play with these ideas.

Slowly come up to surface awareness.

Findings: Document your Findings. This means to simply document, preferably in writing, what comes to you during the course of the exercise, positive, negative or in between. It is important to document these mental experiences, in order to ground them and make them physical. It also allows you to consult your Findings during and at the end of the Reality Creation project, so that you may make plans for future projects.

If each day, or week, or phase of the moon teaches a Lesson, what was the Lesson for today or this week or this phase of the moon?

Chapter 2

The Best Case Scenario

*"A deep appreciation of the current moment
reveals that you have already arrived
at your destination."*

One of my Students: During a session with a student who was attempting to contact the spirit of her transitioned mother, I suggested that contact was already made long ago. I noted that each time she remembered her mother fondly, with Loving Understanding, that she WAS communicating with the transitioned Soul of this human. Indeed, I explained, this is how communications begin and continue. "The next step is to ask for replies to your questions," I suggested. In a short time, she was able to pick up the thread, and hold a loving conversation with her mother.

Your Vision

This is a book on manifesting. As such, we are required to ask you-the-reader to consider what it is you truly want to create. We have called this construct the **Best Case Scenario** in our books. This idealized concept is fueled by desire. It is held aloft on emotional energies, in other words. What is it that you desire most in this world? This is the truth of the matter, you see. This is what you truly wish to have manifested. Then, by considering this construct in its entirety, we have something to go with, in so far as a goal, a Vision for the future.

When you have been honest about what you wish to manifest, your Higher Centers of Awareness begin to immediately find a way to give you what you want. Others have referred to this tendency as The Law of Attraction. However, I do not see the Reality Creator as attracting anything. I do see you as Resonating your world and yourself into being, right where you are now. Thus, perhaps I favor a Law of **Resonance**.

Now this program will work for you to create whatever you have in mind, and I am making a small pun here. For you create your physical reality FIRST, within your consciousness, and THEN you manifest it out into the Third Dimension. So consider what is on your mind in this moment in which you read my words. Is your Best Case Scenario on your mind in this moment?

The Pre-manifestation Domain

Your Best Case Scenario is composed of many positive, pleasurable elements. However it is still an etheric concept at this time. It may be vague or it may be somewhat "filled in" with your thoughts, images and emotions. Yet it is currently un-manifested, and thus resides on another plane of existence, a probable plane, as I say in my books. Let us assume that this dimensional plane is where realities reside before they emerge into your system. It is a type of "staging area" where your reality is formed before it acquires enough emotional energy to become manifest in the physical dimension. I refer to this etheric locale as the **Pre-manifestation Domain**.

Back Engineering Your BCS

Back Engineering is a term we have borrowed from other disciplines. We have given it our own meaning and our own subtext. Here, by Back Engineering, we mean that the student is so confident that their Vision, the Best Case Scenario, is completed and awaiting manifestation in the Pre-manifestation Domain, that they eagerly look for signs in their current reality that they are going to get what they desire. They invoke intense emotion in their current moments in anticipation of experiencing their Vision, and they direct that emotion energy to the Pre-manifestation Domain. They then begin to receive information in the form of Impulses from their Probable Future Self that is experiencing the Best Case Scenario. This information has to do with what the student has thought, felt, heard, and done in order to create the Vision in the future.

Now this may begin to sound like science fiction. I am aware of that. I encourage you, however, to curb your cynicism and explore these concepts playfully and with an open mind. You may very well find that you are turning science fiction into science fact with these practices.

Please see the

Best Case Scenario Flowchart

on the following page.

BEST CASE SCENARIO FLOWCHART

-- THE FUTURE --

PREMANIFESTATION DOMAIN

BEST CASE SCENARIO

V

IMPULSE

V

-- THE PRESENT --

V

ACTION

V

INSIGHT

Communications flow from the top
to the bottom, from the Future
to the Present Moment. You act
on the impulse from the Future
to support the creation of the BCS
NOW. Afterwards, you have an insight
as to where the impulse orginated.
Insight follows action.

Now EVERYTHING exists in potential, within the Pre-manifestation Domain. Every possible probability is explored there. For this reason, I can assure you that your specific Vision that you have in mind for this manifestation project <u>is there</u> waiting for you in this etheric dimension. All that is required from you is the necessary amount of emotional energy and Intent. This is the trigger that moves the manifestation from the probable into the actual. With that in mind...

Exercise: Unpack Your Vision

Create Sanctuary Now

Have a blank piece of paper in front of you with some pencils and pens to write and draw with at your side. Now close your eyes and enter into a **Light Trance State** through whatever practices suit you. A simple technique that many of my students find effective is to relax in a seated position and focus on your breathing. As you breathe out, allow anxiety and cynicism to flow out with the breath. As you breathe in, allow the natural formative energies of the Universe to come within you to balance and to heal your physical body.

Now that you are relaxed and focused on your Inner World, consider your Vision, the reality you would like to create while reading this book and doing the exercises in it. It will make itself known to you in your favored orientations: visual, tactile, auditory, olfactory or gustatory. In other words, you may see yourself experiencing a healing of your malady, or you may hear your friends congratulating you on your new-found wealth, or you may feel the touch of your Lover's fingers upon your skin. Assure yourself that you will retain photographic memories of what transpires in this Light Trance State.

When you have received your information, open your eyes and slowly come up to surface awareness.

Findings: Immediately write down what you experienced. Be as thorough and illustrative as you can be in your documentation. Draw pictures if that helps you. Describe all sensory stimuli you experienced while doing this exercise.

The Censor Speaks

Now read this document over to yourself. Is something coming up for you? Are your Issues being triggered, Dear Reader?

Immediately what often occurs is this: the thought emerges as to how "deserving" you might be of such treasures as this Vision of yours. Also there may appear questions of how much time and possibly work, energy, and so on, will be required to achieve it. Let me allow you to circumvent all of these censoring and dis-empowering thought-forms and images with another exercise, in which you will access your highest creative self...

What gave you pleasure as a child? What filled your consciousness with ecstasy when you were young, before you were socialized, before you where told to grow up? Put your focus there, and we shall begin this next exercise...

The Magical Child Speaks: Playing with Your Beliefs

Create Sanctuary Now

Take out a piece of paper and draw a line down the center of it, dividing the paper into two columns. Write down in the right hand column the doubts you have about your Project. Now it is my assertion that these doubts come from an aspect of your identity we call the Ego/Intellect. This perception does not want you to change the status quo. It becomes agitated and afraid when you consider radical change such as this self-improvement Project.

The Ego will tell you that you don't deserve it, because of etc. etc. etc. The Intellect will present reasons about how it is best for you to remain just the way you are, and not "rock the boat" with ideas of transforming your world.

The Ego/Intellect, also called The Censor, deals in limiting beliefs. You are attempting to change your belief system. Yes that is true. And you may be finding some success with instilling positive beliefs into your consciousness, through using my system or other systems of personal growth. However, you may still be operating from within the old system that sees Lack, difficulty and punishment as the rewards for assuming the Creator Role. Do you see how religious programming may enter in here as the culprit, as the spoiler of fun and excitement for you?

Now do not sweep these unfortunate images, emotions and thoughts under the metaphorical rug of consciousness as they come up. Do you see how that is the problem? Denial and repression is the problem, here.

Acknowledge the Negative

Dear Reader, first <u>do</u> see these negative thought forms, images and emotions in their harsh reality without flinching, without repressing, without "accidentally forgetting." If you have been unable to come up with some negative material until now, BRING IT UP NOW. Each of you has these emotional barriers to self-realization. Bring them up now and write them down in the right hand column. Then please note how these notions of limitation have kept you from experiencing pleasure, success and Love in your life. I would like you to sit with that suggestion for just a few moments...

Now fortunately for you, there is another aspect of your greater identity that <u>does</u> want positive change, that <u>will</u> provide positive reasons for you to awaken. In fact this aspect of your consciousness will be your greatest support in the coming weeks of manifesting. We call this perspective of Reality Creation the Magical Child.

Close your eyes and enter into a Light Trance State.

Embody the **Magical Child** now, by allowing your consciousness to drift back in time to that point in your life when you were allowed to just be a child. You had no responsibilities. You played throughout the day. You were a prolific reality creator and you specialized in fun realities. You believed in magic and you used magic to create entertaining realities for yourself and your friends.

As you tune-in to that part of your life, you may begin to hear, see, and feel the world as you experienced it back then. You are there.

Now open your eyes as the Magical Child, and while still in a Light Trance State, in the left hand column, spend a few minutes writing down the positive elements of your Project. Perhaps you would list fun things you will do when your Project is successful, or perhaps list items you will buy when you create abundance. Will you enjoy positive physical pursuits when you are feeling better? Be thorough in listing these elements just as you were thorough in listing the "dangers."

Your Beliefs

Dear Reader, these are ALL your beliefs. All of this material, the positive and the negative, represents your beliefs. Remember, you use your beliefs about what is possible, to create your physical body and your Personal Reality Field. Thus, I would guess that this list of the positive and the negative aspects of your achieving your Vision also fairly reflects the state of your Personal Reality as a whole. It makes sense, does it not, that if you are being forthright and Courageous as you list these elements of your belief system, that the "causes" of your Negative Realities would show themselves quite dramatically? Indeed, to the degree that you are being honest and Courageous in this exercise, you will also discover the hidden Truth about who you are and why you are on Earth at this time.

Obviously, some of this material will cause pain, shame and other Negative Emotions: the material in the right hand column. But the revelations in the left hand column of this exercise sheet point to other Truths, to the astounding strengths and potentials within your identity that are possibly just now coming into view.

Now play with those positive beliefs for a few minutes. It may help to close your eyes again. As a child would, act out the empowered roles of Entrepreneur, Great Lover, Great Healer, Courageous Leader, and so on. As the Magical Child, perform these powerful roles, just as a child would, with gusto, with great pleasure. Be successful now, Dear Reader. If you are the captain of your ship, as we say in our books, act as though you are the captain of your ship. Envision yourself as healthy, wealthy, wise and happy NOW.

And please save those Negative Findings of the Censor Ego/Intellect for a later date in this program. (See **The Box**.) We will show you how to transform these negatives into positives.

Slowly come up to surface awareness.

Findings: Document your Findings.

Your Mythic Quest

You may know that I see these personal Regimens that my students create and follow, in somewhat romantic and mythic terms. For it IS necessary to imbue your activities in these matters with strong emotion, symbolism, a subtext of personal liberation. For this reason, I am not shy about suggesting that my students embellish these ritual enactments with their private material, the personal material of visions, dreams, wishes, desires, fantasies. It does take a visionary perspective to dream up a potent Reality Creation Project, and then enact it in the Personal Reality Field.

Your Vision Statement: What would be a perfect outcome?

You are the Visionary. Write down on a piece of paper in a few sentences or in a series of steps or phases what you would like to create. Include all elements of your perfect Vision.

The New Moon

I suggest you begin your project during the New Moon. You are a human being with a history. The history of your race is one of appreciating the passage of the moon and the sun in the sky. This perception of the transiting of heavenly bodies quite naturally grounds you in Natural Time. The ancient humans recognized this new moon phase as one of celestial beginnings. It was obvious to the ordinary observer, that during this phase of the 28 day lunar cycle, Mother Nature was preparing to "grow" the moon. This ordinary citizen recognized their connection to the lunar cycle. You could say that they identified personally with the moon, the sun and the stars in this way. If you can remember this identification with something greater than yourself – the moon, the stars, the flashes of light in the nighttime sky – you will go a long way toward experiencing this Natural Time that I am referencing.

The Path Reversed: Begin at the End

Now then, as we move towards implementing your plan, we are going to turn on its head the Travel Metaphor we have used so often. In the past I have suggested that the student conceive of their Regimen as a Journey, a Trip. I suggested that they begin at the beginning and work their way toward a conclusion, or destination of some sort, gathering Findings along the way. That suited us at the time, for you were new to my Teaching and you required the basics. Now you have mastered the basics and I am able to ask for you to begin, not at the beginning, **but at the end**, the destination.

The Path Reversed is an essential metaphor, Dear Reader. As such, it holds a certain charge, a magical charge if you will, for you the Practitioner. This suggestion is one of my reminders to you of the **Ancient Wisdom** precepts. Over the course of reading this book, as you learn more and more about the subtext of this potent idea, I believe that you may begin to experience the essence of this concept. As you do you will find yourself in an Altared State of consciousness, one in which you begin to "see with new eyes." You will in fact be quite able, over time, to discern from any particular current moment in your existence, what you may focus on in order to create your **Best Case Scenario**, your Vision, you see. In fact, you may find that a deep appreciation of the current moment reveals that you have already arrived at your destination.

After a few days of actually <u>believing</u> this essential metaphor, you begin to receive information from the Probable Future on what was done <u>by you</u> to create this ideal state. From the Pre-manifestation Domain comes this information that becomes subtly evident in your current moments of Reality Creation in the form of Impulses. It is realized as a type of portending. You may experience sensory precursors that make themselves known as intriguing thoughts, feelings, visual images and emotions that literally tug at your perceptions. In a sense, they "want" to tell you something. They want to prepare you for achieving your BCS.

The Full Moon is Implied in the New

With regards to this Best Case Scenario, the full moon is <u>implied</u> in the darkness of the new moon. Because you are this human with a history and a knowledge of the Ancient Wisdom, and because you have experienced countless lunar and solar cycles in your many lives, you are assured and confident of the eventual arrival of the full brilliant moon, right on time, so to speak, even though you are experiencing the darkness of the moon currently.

In the same exact way, as you look at your Reality Creation Project now in the beginning of this process, your dream, your Vision, your Best Case Scenario is implied in this new moon. Do you see? This is the magical state of consciousness that you embody to manifest the end result <u>now</u>, in your current moment within Natural Time. Please appreciate the subtext of this statement, and then read on Dear Reader.

Anything Is Possible

As you begin your Manifestation Project, please know that ANYTHING is possible. You may create whatever you wish. All of the separate elements of your dream that you identified as composing your Vision Statement are achievable, Dear Reader. This means that the sum of all of these elements, the Best Case Scenario, is possible, or, quite probable, as I say in my books. Knowing you are assured of success...

Begin your Trip

You have put together some ideas on paper. You have noted where improvements may be made in your Reality Creation. Without stress and without urgency but with high motivation and confidence, you begin. If you find yourself initially lacking this required enthusiasm, that is quite common. Do not let that dissuade you from beginning your Quest. Often, the fervor and dedication, the commitment and strength, are generated over time, you see, over the course of your Project. In the beginning phase, you may tread lightly on this path of yours.

End of Chapter Assignments

Using Back Engineering, identify 3 signs from your current reality that you will be successful in your Reality Creation Project <u>and write them down</u>.

If each day, or week, or phase of the moon teaches a Lesson, what was the Lesson for to-day, or this week or this phase of the moon?

Days 9-12
Crescent Moon
Facilitate

Chapter 3
The Telepathic Network

*"The Telepathic Network contains
the electromagnetic 'glue' that holds
your reality together."*

One of my Students: I was having some difficulty with a student of mine at one of our workshops. She was struggling with the notion that everything in your system is composed of Consciousness Units, including your physical body and everything else. I then related to her my Holographic Insert **When You Walk Across the Room**. As she told me later, this teaching story allowed her to experience herself as a metaphor or divine expression of her Entity, of her Soul, and of All That Is. She had a small awakening, and began to smile.

Telepathic Network

Here we have another essential metaphor, one that <u>displays</u> the veritable essence or truth of the subject matter. This descriptive form is ripe with subtext, as I have also described to you earlier. And again, this subtext, this "hidden meaning," becomes known only when you-the-reader expand your beliefs to account for it.

I shall be blunt. Here with this idea of a Telepathic Network, I, Seth, am inviting you to participate with me in communications on the subtle levels within the Unknown Reality. This is the network that I use to communicate with ALL of my students. This etheric structure reveals to the awakening student the ongoing transformation of thought, image and emotion into Reality Constructs. The Telepathic Network contains the electromagnetic elements - the Consciousness Units, or CU's - that hold your reality together and make instant communication possible.

To be awake in this system of communication gives you an edge. You see how things work. You begin to sense when the time is right to intervene with your thoughts, images, emotions and behaviors to further your goals and to implement your Vision

Statement. To be awake in the Telepathic Network also connects you directly with your Guides. The non-physical beings will make themselves known to you through this etheric network.

Practical Applications

The realization, when it comes to you, that you are actually an artist submerged in your own medium - the Consciousness Units - that you are the artist and the work of art simultaneously, can be very liberating, "empowering," as they say. In terms of practical applications for the work at hand, let me say this...

You Are Already Manifesting

Your manifestation project will begin to succeed when you realize that your ongoing existence is already one of momentary manifesting. You are already creating your current moments, in other words, one after the other. You do it naturally and subconsciously for the most part, and so you may find that you are experiencing some Negative Realities within this reflexive, responsive Telepathic Network. The CU's literally mirror on the outside all of the ongoing thoughts, images, and emotions you are experiencing within your conscious and subconscious mind.

Momentary Awakenings

After you have begun your Journey, with your plan in hand, still you may be met with resistance. Still it may be difficult to make progress. Then, with that realization, it becomes necessary to awaken in the current moments of your reality.

Negative ruminations, otherwise known as negative circular thoughts, are the foundation of Negative Realities. If you are encountering resistance and other obstacles on your path to your Best Case Scenario, consider what is on your mind as you identify these resistances and these obstacles. What you are thinking about at these times of negatively assessing your environment are these "reasons," these negative ruminations. As you think these circular thoughts, automatically they become manifest before you, because you, Dear Reader, are creating them. You are creating out of the CU's before you, the physical manifestation of these mental constructs, the circular thoughts.

Now when you first catch yourself doing this, it will come as a major revelation. You may find yourself bursting into laughter. This is the secret, you see. This is the proof to yourself that you create your own Personal Reality. It comes as a momentary awakening, in that, because it is so preposterous, astounding and unbelievable, your Ego/Intellect may force you to turn away, to minimize this revelation, to immediately forget and repress it. It only lasts a second, but the damage to the Ego's credibility is already done. There is no turning back after this awakening in the moment. The transformation has begun.

Continuous Gratitude

Continuous gratitude, from my perspective, is your most effective tool in your Reality Creation Project, for you are always Back Engineering your Best Case Scenario in this way. Let me elaborate for a bit... With grateful positive expectation, you are continuously anticipating a positive result, evidence of your BCS, let us say. This is a form of **Consecutive Positive Assessments** that we have described in our past books. You are pulling from all data available to you, only the supportive elements in your environment. Bad news has no place here, in other words. You are always, Dear Reader, gratefully noticing and focusing on your anticipated positive result, whatever that may be. You then begin to see it emerge into your world.

There often come these synchronicities, the harbingers of success. You notice and give thanks for them and increase your Loving focus. Also, anticipating synchronicities helps to create them. Let me make my point here... You get what you focus on. If you are looking for information from your environment that suggests you are getting what you want, you begin to find that information. Proof is what you are finding.

Breakdown or Breakthrough?

Another technique to employ while you are navigating your Reality Creation Journey is this simple option that you present to yourself in times of perceived frustration and disappointment: Is it a breakdown or a breakthrough, Dear Reader? Are you falling apart or coming together? The assessment is up to you.

Make the decision, therefore, to act in the positive arena, for your benefit, to support your Vision. In fact, within each successive moment of your waking reality, you have these opportunities to select which way you would like to go. If you would like to move forward, and fulfill the criteria in your Vision Statement, the choice becomes obvious: perceive and create your breakthrough and coming together moments. However, if you would like to continue the status quo of perhaps stasis, stagnation, despair and powerlessness, then your choice might be to break down and fall apart.

Multitasking

I am having a humorous moment with you, here, yet I am quite serious with my Intent. By correcting your own mis-perceptions in the moment, and then witnessing these amendments to your Personal Reality made manifest in the next few moments - Instant Manifestation, you see - you are riding the cutting edge of Reality Creation. You are at these times **multi-tasking**, as we say in the books. You are straddling the physical and the metaphysical domains. You are being guided by your Higher Centers of Awareness, even as you may be functioning seemingly quite normally at work, or in normal conversations with friends and family. You are, in fact, maintaining your "normal" Third-Dimensional persona while receiving communications from your Guides, from All That Is, from your Future Probable Self.

Telepathic and Holographic

Put another way... when you are on the edge of creating in the Back Engineering mode, you are outside of linear time. Please remember my model for consciousness that includes the Consciousness Units that represent telepathic holographic communication energy. Now telepathy implies instant communication between consciousness identities, humans, if you will, yet also everything else, for all is conscious. Holography implies the All within each particle, each CU. Thus, here in this Altared State, you already know the outcome of your Project. You may observe the timeline, beginning with Day 1 and ending with Day 28. Project your consciousness deeper into this construct and see for yourself what you have done to create your Best Case Scenario.

Now your Vision is one of innumerable probabilities that you may manifest. Yet you are focusing on this Vision rather than the other probabilities, for you are attempting to manifest an improvement in your Reality Creation. It is important here to not sell yourself short, I believe, out of some sense of misplaced humility. Look for and find the images, the sensory inputs, behaviors, the people, places, things and events that you require to realize your Vision.

Vitalize Your Beliefs

Are you vitalizing your beliefs with enough emotional energy that they will seek manifestation in your Personal Reality Field? You will know you are on the right track when you begin to feel your Vision manifesting in front of you. Now this is not as outlandish as you might think. Everyone has had moments of being psychically tuned-in to their environment so that they "just knew" what was going to happen in the next few moments, minutes or hours. And then it happened.

Create Sanctuary Now

On a piece of paper, draw a line down the middle dividing the paper into two columns. In the left hand column list what you feel are the positive beliefs that you hold, that will help you to create your Best Case Scenario. In this column you might put, "I am a powerful person, I can stand up to my boss and ask for the raise." "I have the power to heal my pancreas, and I am doing so NOW." "I intuitively understand what is the most beneficial action for me to take in each moment, and I take that action."

In the right hand column, next to the statement of positive belief, write down a few descriptive words that support the belief. Next to the phrase "I am a powerful person, I can stand up to my boss and ask for the raise," you might put the emotive words STRONG ABUNDANT COURAGEOUS WORTHY LOVING etc.

The next step involves magnifying the emotional subtext of the words in the right hand column. As you recite these words, mentally or verbally, you instill within your consciousness the accompanying feelings of positive emotion. You are embodying these positive emotions, Dear Reader, as you conduct this exercise. Now whenever you read your belief statements to yourself, they will virtually ring with this charge of emotional content. This is the charged subtext of the belief that your subconscious will respond to whenever you read this statement. This emotional charge may be used to help push your manifestation into the physical plane. On the surface, it looks as though you are reciting an affirmation about yourself. Within the Telepathic Network, however, the emotional charge is assisting in the creation of the new reality you are affirming.

Findings: Document your Findings.

End of Chapter Assignments

Using Back Engineering, identify 3 signs from your current reality that you will be successful in your Reality Creation Project <u>and write them down</u>.

If each day, or week, or phase of the moon teaches a Lesson, what was the Lesson for today, or this week or this phase of the moon?

Days 13-16
First Quarter Moon
Thrive

Chapter 4
Picking Up the Trail

*"When you find something interesting
put it in your bag."*

One of my Students: "Your Issue is what forces you to go on the Path of Awakening," I said to my young student. "But I don't have any Issues. I have been in psychotherapy for several years." Then I said, "Perhaps your Issue is that you do not think you have Issues. But if you have no Issues, why did you go into therapy?" "Oh, I get it." she replied, smiling. "I'm an Issue denier." Thus, the denial is broken.

Metaphorical Tools: The Bag and The Box

You are most likely well on your way in this project of yours, and meeting with some successes and possibly some experiences that appear less successful. Now I would like to offer you two very powerful technologies to use to sort out these mixed Findings.

Exercise:

The Bag

The Bag is a **Metaphorical Tool** that you may use in your investigations into your Personal Reality. If you are engaged in creating a Best Case Scenario as we suggest in this book, consider this tool as a type of filing cabinet or secure storage container. Just as you would store in your safe any valuables or keep-sakes you might own, just as you might find it convenient to file away important papers in your filing cabinet, use this visualized bag to store positive experiences that you enjoy in your waking or dreaming worlds.

Create Sanctuary Now

Close your eyes and enter into a Light Trance State. You may wish to visualize a dial that you may turn to dial-in the precise frequency you require to create the Metaphorical Tools. Your creative consciousness will take you there if you allow it. Now The Bag may be any type of bag that you have seen in your life. Imagine that you see such a bag now. Imagine that it is suspended around your neck, or perhaps tied around your waist somehow. Position the bag so that it is handy and accessible. Now see yourself having a pleasant experience, with regards to your Reality Creation Project. You are experiencing success, in other words. If you are on a Path of Abundance, and you are experiencing an increase in monetary flow, see yourself placing this good news in your Metaphorical Bag. See yourself going about implementing your project in your world, and when you find something interesting put it in your bag. Now see yourself examining the contents of this etheric bag at regular intervals throughout your Project, for inspiration and for affirmation, that you are on a productive path of self development.

Open your eyes and slowly come up to surface awareness.

Findings: Document your Findings.

Exercise:
The Box

We first spoke of The Box in my book on 911. Briefly, this Metaphorical Tool is one that turns "poison into medicine." The poisons we are referring to are the Negative Findings that you discover during your Manifestation Project. It is an etheric box that exists in your creative imagination. The Box is formed, such that it transforms negatives into positives. How can this be so? You create your reality. It becomes a fact, for you identify it as a fact. In fact, you enlarge your belief system to include magic, my friend. In this sense, it is a magic box of transformation.

Create Sanctuary Now

Close your eyes and create a Light Trance State. As you did with The Bag Exercise, have your consciousness dial-in the precise frequency for you to experience The Box. Now Imagine yourself experiencing a negative event in your reality. But rather than reacting negatively to the event by becoming upset, let's say, or angry or fearful, simply place that event and all of the participants in The Box. Do this with your imagination, knowing that, in time, the energies of transformation will turn the event into a positive one. You may even put the transformation on a schedule, by saying to yourself, "This event will be transformed into a positive Lesson for me in only two weeks time," or some such thing. Then, when the time has arrived, you open The Box and surprise yourself by seeing that it has been transformed into its opposite. Again, you have enlarged your belief system to include magic.

Open your eyes and slowly come up to surface awareness.

Findings: Document your Findings.

Negotiating

I use the term negotiating to describe this process of the human on a Path of Transformation making their way IN SPITE of the protests and the self-sabotaging efforts of the Ego/Intellect. Yes, you will be negotiating with these aspects of your Identity. You may find yourself having to reassure your Ego, for example, that you are not abandoning it when you work diligently for change of your status quo reality. You may of necessity have to ignore, sometimes, the elaborate reasons and excuses of your Intellect when it presents the facts and figures, as to why you are on a dangerous and perhaps futile journey. Yes, you may have to give in a little to receive more cooperation, or at least a silencing of this inner dialogue of despair. Yet, this is how your ultimate Vision is formed, in this negotiation between the Ego, the Intellect and your Higher Centers of Awareness.

Holding on and Letting Go: The Manifestation Dynamic

This dynamic, that you could also call Taking Charge and Surrendering, constitutes the underlying energy system of the conscious manifestation process, in my view. When you are consciously creating your world, as you are now Dear Reader, you are connected to your Source, and you have the vast support system that this entails. You are connected to the communication stream of All That Is, possibly your own individualized Guides of various types, and other of the non-physical beings. These energy bodies constitute your "entourage," so to speak, as you function within the etheric world.

Automatic Creation

In the physical world, however, it may seem that you are on your own. Indeed, you are within each moment of your waking reality, faced with a multitude of decisions that you alone must make, just to keep the status quo reality intact. Yes, the majority of these decisions are made automatically by your unconscious. Your body, for example, is made manifest moment-to-moment within the CU's that comprise this vehicle of yours. And the various Reality Constructs that populate your environment - trees, automobiles, mountains, buildings - are also spontaneously and automatically re-created moment-to-moment within the electromagnetic influences of the Telepathic Network. Most of your reality, then, is spontaneously created, without the need for conscious input from you.

Yet you are now on a Journey of Manifestation in which you are attempting to change the status quo for you personally. Beyond this automatic reality exists your Identity and those choices you make using your Free-Will. These will determine what you will create in succeeding moments. This is a somewhat drawn out prelude to this important explanation...

Through Holding on, through Taking Charge, through Assessing in the Moment, through observing your reality and looking for signs that you are succeeding, you literally change what you are observing. Your perception creates reality in your dimension. (See the **Percept**.) In this way, the Letting Go, the other half of this dynamic, is a type of re-fresh function with this reality of yours, in that, as you consciously surrender, after you have made your changes in your reality in the Holding On mode, you allow your reality to re-create itself to reveal the improved reality.

Obsession and Neglect

Now by over-emphasizing either side of this energy dynamic, you may wind up in difficulties. A light touch is required at all times. **For example**: If you become overly invested in your project, to the degree that you are obsessed with finding the positive in your Reality Creation efforts, and you in fact create a stranglehold on your reality, your creations become stilted and without life. You are forgetting to allow the natural forces to assist you by surrendering appropriately.

On the other hand, when you are too focused on surrendering and Letting Go, you are neglecting to provide your valuable direction in this process. Your creations, therefore, have a tendency to spread out and becomes less precise. It would appear to you, perhaps, that you are not making as much progress in your project as you had hoped. Do you see?

When do you surrender, then? When you feel it is the right time. As you work within Natural Time, taking a cue from the moon and sun and all of the natural signs you see in your Personal Reality, you become aware of when it is time to Let Go, to stop assessing. Yes, this entire dynamic of Holding On and Letting Go may play out numerous times throughout one day. The idea is to become aware of it so that you can direct it for your own benefit.

Dear Reader, the Negative Realities that you create endure and re-create themselves automatically. For this reason you ask yourself at various points through-out your waking days and nights, "Am I focusing obsessively on one side of this dynamic in this current moment?" Then you have a choice, you see. Then you have an opportunity to break this Trance of automatic Negative Reality Creation, and intervene.

Becoming Comfortable in the New Consciousness

All of these techniques are offered to you in the hope that you will use them to become comfortable in the New Consciousness in which you find yourself. If you have read this far into our little book, I would suggest that you are already in the New Consciousness, at least somewhat. You cannot help yourself, you see. These words of mine have a certain rhythm and a certain subtext that allows the average reader to go within and discover this new way of perceiving and experiencing we call the New Consciousness. It is really a new dimension that you are becoming acquainted with, as you begin to read and attempt to comprehend what I am describing.

Now the degree to which you can be comfortable and even powerful within the New Consciousness will determine how successful you are with your exploits, with your Reality Creation Projects. Therefore, I suggest you commit to an appreciation for this path of understanding.

Exercise:
Deep Appreciation

I will now tie gratitude in with my premise that your Best Case Scenario may be Back Engineered through a <u>full</u> appreciation of your current **Moment Point**. Now I am using the word **appreciation** in a unique way, here. A full appreciation of your current moment would allow you to perceive exactly what you need to do, see, hear, say, smell and touch in order to experience the desired outcome. Then, as these elements of manifestation "come to mind," you show gratitude, appreciation, you see, for the gift from Self, from Spirit. This form of appreciation is an Altared State of perception that is powered and extended by your gratitude in the moment.

This is a skill, this learned expression of immediate thankfulness upon receiving the communications from your future evolved Self. The doubting Intellect and the astounded Ego are sidestepped in this appreciation process. You are devoted to expressing thanks for the information you are receiving, here. Additionally, it feels good in this moment of appreciation. You are experiencing contact with your Higher Centers of Awareness and so ecstasy prevails. If fear or anxiety arises, gently counsel your Ego/Intellect that you are not abandoning them. You are simply witnessing an enlarged, more comprehensive view of your Personal Reality. That is all.

Gratitude is the appropriate response, always. When you can be grateful for even a negative experience, you may begin to experience Momentary Awakenings. Are you grateful now? Ask yourself this question at various intervals throughout the day. An example is in order...

Loving What Is AND What You Want

Let us say that your goal is to manifest a new car, for your current vehicle is becoming less and less reliable and road-worthy. How do you accomplish this? From my perspective, you maintain a multi-tasking awareness, here. You drive your current vehicle in a state of Good Humor <u>always</u>. You are good natured about the deficits of this car. You appreciate the service that your car is giving you now and has given you in the past. It is a pleasant mutually satisfying relationship you have with this car, you see. You attend to the needs of the car, through providing oil and coolant and the odd repairs. The car reciprocates, in a way, by continuing to provide transportation for you.

Creating Lack

What you do not want to do is what many people do in this circumstance. Many people complain about the failing car and swear at the failing car and DO NOT appreciate the car for its service up to that point. By complaining, you sustain the current Negative Reality of "failing car." You allow the concept of failing car to continue into the future by complaining about it in your current moments of

Reality Creation. It is a form of Lack creation that many people engage in subconsciously. Often, it takes an aware observer to tell these people what they are doing to themselves, i.e., they are re-creating Lack moment-to-moment.

This is one side of the multitasking Good Humor state of consciousness. The other aspect is this: you desire, you require, you anticipate having a new car to replace your current vehicle, for it has problems that are not solvable. Then, even as you create Good Humor around the relationship with your current vehicle, you are also creating space within your Personal Reality Field for the new vehicle to emerge. In this way, you are Loving what you have currently, while, at the same time, looking for signs of the manifestation of the new car. This is what you do when you multitask with Good Humor.

Trends in Conscious Co-creation

Another inclination of consciousness you may notice, while you are attempting to roll-out your Project in physical reality, is for your creations to assume particular and consistent forms of expression. These are simply broad generalizations we can make, with regards to how your efforts are becoming manifest in your Personal Reality Field.

The power of these assessments lies in the assessments themselves. By identifying a trend or tendency in your creative pursuits, you are immediately giving it creative energy in the moment. (See the **Percept**.) Thus, it does not do to assess negatively, here, for you will merely sustain the Negative Reality in those moments. My suggestion is that you identify these trends with neutral emotion and give them non-threatening names.

Two Steps Forward and One Step Back
One Step Forward and Two Steps Back

Two Steps Forward and One Step Back is a common trend in the manifestation process. This tendency in conscious co-creation sees the Practitioner moving ahead with their Project, guided by their Vision Statement and making steady progress, but with regular setbacks. It seems that each time progress is made, something occurs that brings the project to a halt, and erodes much of the forward progress. During this phase, it is important to remember that you are making <u>some</u> progress. Your efforts are having a positive effect. Simply knowing that this phenomenon is quite common, and often tempo-rary, helps to maintain motivation, to continue the Reality Creation Project.

The companion to this inclination of consciousness we call One Step Forward and Two Steps Back. Here the creator finds themselves continuously los-ing ground in their efforts to create their improved realities. One step forward, in which some gains are made, is immediately followed by two steps back, in which those gains are eliminated and even more is lost. The situation is worse than before the Prac-titioner began the Program. In this case it is doubly important to name this phenomenon innocuously, and not perceive failure, danger, hopelessness, and so on. By identifying it, again, as a common, tem-porary occurrence in these practices, faith and mo-tivation are maintained.

Example:
You Get What You Focus On

Suppose you are eagerly moving forward with your Project. You have settled on something you want to create, whatever that may be. Because you are human, it may take some time to concentrate your focus so that you can find the connections. But then one moment it dawns on you what I am talking about. You have a little awakening in your mental arena. As you look around, you DO see the connections between "normal" Reality Constructs, friends, events, what have you, and the desired outcome: the manifestation. Might I say that you begin to see the connections, the positive connections, because you are committed to finding them and focusing on them? Yet usually you do receive these communications from the future in small increments. These are teasers to keep you on the path, so to speak. You may say that you are testing yourself at these times. You are testing your commitment to consciousness change. Other signals from your probable future confirm your ultimate success. Finally you gratefully receive your manifestation in its totality via your perception in the moment.

End of Chapter Assignments

Using Back Engineering, identify 3 signs from your current reality that you will be successful in your Reality Creation Project <u>and write them down</u>.

If each day, or week, or phase of the moon teaches a Lesson, what was the Lesson for today, or this week or this phase of the moon?

Days 17-20
Gibbous Moon
Realize

Chapter 5
Getting Lost

*"To become a child again, let go and be carried
by the flow of the natural world."*

One of my Students: Our students who have experienced trauma in their childhood may have a
difficult time accessing the state of consciousness
we call the Magical Child perspective. One of these
students was angrily describing to me how it was
necessary to be eternally vigilant, so that he would
not be taken advantage of by friends, family and
co-workers. I suggested to him that he was still
viewing and thus creating his reality from the perspective of the abused child. "What would it take

for you to completely surrender to that Magical Child that existed prior to the abuse?" He took a deep breath.

Dropping the Ego/Intellect

At this stage of your Project you may be experiencing the benefits of synchronizing with the moon and the natural energies of the Earth. With this contact often comes a desire to completely let go of the timetables, the techniques, the Project itself. From my perspective, this is a very natural stage in the process, when the work itself demands a dramatic change. In this Practice we often speak of the metaphorical reset button. In this case, success demands that the Reality Creator let go of the Program and Procedures of the Reality Creation Project temporarily, to allow the new Identity to coalesce and solidify. It is time for a change, in other words. We call it Getting Lost. The technique involves dropping the Ego/Intellect completely so that you can witness what changes must be made to complete your Project successfully.

Getting Lost is a specialty of The Magical Child. Just as a child may be brutally honest, speaking the truth though it may be uncomfortable for others, when you are perceiving as the Magical Child, you see the Truth of your Project up to this point. You see what is missing. You do not have the Ego/Intellect confusing you. You are able to see what must be done to succeed.

Exercise:
Wondering Wandering
and Getting Lost

Now achieving the Getting Lost level of understanding and staying there for minutes and hours may take some doing. It may be best to attempt this part of the Project when you have some time off, on the weekends, or at other times when you can invoke the Magical Child safely and without interference.

In our book **Resonance** we speak of the virtues of wondering, and the value in allowing your consciousness to regularly drift without direction and without anxiety. The state of consciousness we call wondering does NOT have expectations. When you approach this Altared State, therefore, please forget about the advice we have given you previously, suggesting that you keep your Vision in mind continuously. Here we ask that you take a respite from the vigilance of the previous exercises, and simply Let Go.

Wandering is a valuable use of your time also, as you attempt to Get Lost. Again, think of what the child does at play, wandering wherever the impulse to wander takes them. This talent is acceptable for a child, yet it has been expelled out of consciousness in the adult. Discover in this Exercise the lost art of wondering, wandering and Getting Lost.

Create Sanctuary Now

Close your eyes and invoke your Light Trance State. Now consider your experiences in creating the Magical Child Perspective from an earlier chapter. The Censor is absent here. The Ego/Intellect has been assured that all is safe and sound. As we have said, to become a child again, let go and be carried by the flow of the natural world. Then, concentrating on your breath, feel yourself surrendering all physical concerns with each breath that you take. It may now be possible for you to achieve the Light Trance State in a few moments of focus and concentration on your Inner World.

Wondering is what the child does when they are looking at the clouds in the day time sky or the stars in the night time sky. Wondering transports your consciousness into the center of the Universe. Here you have no agenda, yet you are privy to the meanings of life. You are connected quite innocently to your Higher Centers of Awareness in this wondering mode.

Now you may begin to smile lightly. You are there. Give yourself the suggestion that you will remember the **Feeling-Tones** experienced in this exercise. The pleasant emotions and other sensory stimuli experienced in the Feeling-Tones are the valuable take-aways from this exercise.

Wandering is easily done in this state. Allow your consciousness to simply go where it will, without direction. Images and sounds from childhood may arise. This is an indication you are on the right track.

Getting Lost, as we define it, is a pleasant task. You have no destination, for you are wandering. You are simply enjoying the sensory stimuli that come when you have no agenda, nothing to accomplish, nothing to worry about.

Open your eyes again and slowly come up to surface awareness.

Findings: Document as best you can the Feeling-Tones you experienced during the exercise.

Benefits of Getting Lost

Certainly, you will have to come out of this state to attend to the business of living. We do not suggest that you spend the bulk of your time Getting Lost. Yet if you are successful with creating the Getting Lost state of consciousness regularly, over the following next few days, during this phase of the moon and of your Project, ideas, images, thoughts of various kinds pertinent to your Project will appear in your mental environment. These impulses to think, feel, and act in particular ways are the messages from your progressed self, the one that enjoys the Best Case Scenario. You are indeed seeing your world through new eyes, here.

As your Identity settles, so to speak, after these psychological interventions, the tendency is to integrate around the few common powerful ideas, images and emotions that were the focus of your consciousness prior to the intervention. Thus, we would see your Identity coming together around the key concepts of Love, Courage, Abundance, spiritual awakening, personal empowerment and the other subjects of your Reality Creation Project.

Filling in the Blanks

This dynamic was also covered in our book **Resonance**. Take your Findings from the Getting Lost exercise, including the material that trickles in during the next few days. Now I realize I may sound like a broken record, here, when I continually emphasize the Path Reversed theory. However, this is indeed the magic of my system. Thus you would assemble this material that represents messages from your future self, from the Pre-manifestation Domain, on what images, ideas, emotions and circular thoughts YOU may embody to be successful in your Reality Creation Project. This is what is missing and you are Filling in the Blanks with this information. The list may be short or long. Edit this material into action statements, so that you can immediately follow your own orders, and institute these changes in your Reality Creation efforts.

Example: Filling in the Blanks

On the premise that the impulses coming into your consciousness are from this Pre-manifestation Domain, you value them and write them down when they come to mind. Some of these messages may be fairly straight forward. They may take the form of directions or suggestions to go to certain locations or to enact certain behaviors. Others may appear nonsensical, at first. Ask your Source about the validity of all of these messages. If you get the go-ahead from your Source, and you have validated this information, my suggestion is to act on this material. It is in the doing that you discover the meanings of these communications from your Future Probable Self. (See the chart on the **BCS**.) By acting on this guidance from the future, you are Filling in the Blanks. You are, theoretically now, amending the Reality Creation Project in beneficial ways. You are increasing your chances of success in this way.

End of Chapter Assignments

Using Back Engineering, identify 3 signs from your current reality that you will be successful in your Reality Creation Project and write them down.

If each day, or week, or phase of the moon teaches a Lesson, what was the Lesson for today, or this week or this phase of the moon?

Days 21-24
Full Moon
Awaken

Chapter 6
Fulfillment

*"What appears to be destiny may be
your personal awakening."*

One of my Students: "I exist outside of time. Here I can see the countless acts of free will from all of your lives that go into the creation of a synchronistic meeting with a potential Soul Mate," I said to my student. "But it is not destiny, by any means. It is a collaboration between your lives and the lives of the potential Soul Mate, that occurs on the etheric plane," I continued. "But to me it's different," she replied. "To me I am fulfilling my destiny by finally finding my Soul Mate." Different metaphors, same phenomenon.

Something Happens Before You Arrive

Dear Reader, what appears to be destiny may be your personal awakening. What are you awakening to? Initially, as you fulfill the criteria in your Vision Statement by establishing your Project in physical reality, you come into contact with your Guides. Those of you who have already developed these relationships will deepen and strengthen them on this Voyage. If you are just now taking the opportunity to meet your Guides, you may be astounded and quite pleased at how close these beings are to you at this time, and how useful they can be in your ongoing attempts to create Positive Realties.

Soul Mate and Soul Family

Additionally, as you awaken at the completion of your Voyage, you become acquainted with Soul Mates and Soul Family members. These people may or may not include what you think of as your true family, your genetic family, your adoptive family, and so on. They are reincarnational colleagues who come into your existence lifetime after lifetime, to learn their Lessons with you. In the same way that you may gradually come into an awareness of your Guides, you may suddenly find yourself, after weeks or months of considering the theories in this manuscript, witnessing not only your current moment experiences with your family, but also the extra-dimensional, past and future life experiences that you have had and will have with your Soul Family members. As I said before, this new perception requires an expansion of belief to initialize it. As with your Guides, you are believing your Soul Mate and Soul Family relationships into existence. You then experience this new dimension as feedback of your growing awareness.

The Library

Now in the beginning it seems as though you are alone. This is true. It seems that you are the dramatist and the sole audience member for the endeavor. Yet soon you find that after you embark upon the mythic quest, generations of other visionaries, those who have gone before, are watching, appreciating, noting your efforts.

These other visionaries who have gone before have contributed to a body of work accessible to you on the Etheric Plane. This Gestalt of Consciousness includes the energy signatures of all humans that have awakened. You, as you awaken during the practicing of the exercises in this book, will add your material to this vast Library of Knowledge, even as you learn from your ancestors how it is done. The term apprenticeship or perhaps adeptship is appropriate here. As you lower your defenses, as you expand your beliefs, as you dig deeper into this material, you are recognized by others, again, even as you recognize the work of these early Practitioners

Now perhaps the word "early" is misleading here. For among the contributions that make up the etheric material of The Library, are those additions from visionaries who have yet to live their lives in your system. These are future Practitioners who nonetheless have informed this Gestalt of Consciousness with their experiences. Future beings, Extra-dimensional energy beings, personalities not completely focused in your reality also contribute to The Library. These Energy Bodies are what some refer to as Masters, Etheric Teachers, and so on. As you connect to The Library, you may get a sense of this class of non-physical beings. They each have their specialty. They each have a particular system they have perfected for achieving the awakened state

I Seth have placed some of my energy in The Library. Just as these Masters of Awakening present their material in separate wings of The Library, you might say, I choose to display this new teaching of mine towards the entrance, so that it may be easy to find. Please note my feeble attempt at humor, Mark.

Mark: OK. Humor noted.

Exercise: Visiting The Library

The Library is there for you to experience, to the degree that you have participated in the exercises in this book. We are not talking about "mastering" these exercises. All that it takes to connect with the Etheric Plane is a consistent practicing of the principles and exercises in this book.

Create Sanctuary Now

Close your eyes and invoke your Light Trance State. In this Trance State, it is a simple matter to anticipate success and to focus on your breath. Feel yourself going somewhat deeper with each breath you take. The Library exists extra-dimensionally, and it is necessary for you to be somewhat more thoroughly relaxed and more focused on your Inner Senses than you were in the previous exercises. Many students of mine experience The Library in purely visual terms. They see a library, perhaps, from their childhood, one with pillars at the entrance, classic architecture, you see. Others view The Library in terms of a felt presence or energy construct, a Feeling-Tone that has several different aspects to it, including the visual, the tactile, the emotional. The Library is there within your mental environment for you to witness in your own time, in your own way. Feel yourself, therefore, drifting towards this construct. It may seem familiar to you, some of these sensations you are feeling. If you are a Seth Entity Human Counterpart, you may have been here before, perhaps, in your early life on the planet in this lifetime or perhaps in other existences, in which you once again were looking for the Truth of your reality.

Now you are there. Look around you and see if there are people in The Library. Introduce yourself if that seems appropriate. Telepathically ask any questions you would like answered.

When you feel the event is concluded, and knowing that you will have complete recall of the experience, open your eyes and slowly return to surface awareness.

Findings: Document your Findings in whatever medium suits you.

Vision Success

This must be said... Each of you will awaken according to your own Issues and Lessons and according to the criteria in your Vision Statement and your Project, broadly speaking. That is, if you are envisioning a return to health from an ongoing malady, for example, you may experience your awakening as a healing of that malady. If you created your Vision Statement around the idea of experiencing an Abundant Universe for yourself, success would possibly be measured in monetary terms. If you are seeking to create an awakening for yourself, an awakening to your life's purpose, let us say, or perhaps a general awakening to the Truth of your reality, success may mean that you are witnessing Truth and Wisdom in your Personal Reality Field. However, if you are now not satisfied with the progress you have made in your Reality Creation Project...

Exercise: Awaken Now

Create Sanctuary Now

Close your eyes and invoke your Light Trance State. These are my suggestions to you at this time. You are either awakening now or you are using denial, intellectualization and other tactics to stay asleep. Either your Higher Centers of Awareness are running things now or your Ego/Intellect is still in charge, for the most part. As you come to the conclusion of your Project, Dear Reader, embody your future probable self that is already an awakened Reality Creator. Embody the self that is already experiencing success, as you understand it, according to the criteria in your Vision Statement. Break the spell of the **Common Trance** NOW and surrender to the **Uncommon Trance** of awakened personal authority and power.

Open your eyes and slowly come up to surface awareness.

Findings: Document your findings. Using your preferred method, document in some way your discoveries in this self-assessment exercise.

End of Chapter Assignments

Using Back Engineering, identify 3 signs from your current reality that you will be successful in your Reality Creation Project <u>and write them down</u>.

If each day, or week, or phase of the moon teaches a Lesson, what was the Lesson for today, or this week or this phase of the moon?

Days 25-28
Disseminating Moon
Share

Chapter 7
Returning

*"Empty your bag and appreciate
the probabilities."*

One of my Students: "But I'm a failure at this Seth. I can't contact my Energy Personality. I can't manifest. I am not getting it," he said over the phone. "Very well, I believe you," I replied. "Now take those very valuable Negative Findings and write them down on the left side of a piece of paper. Now to the right side of each Negative Finding write its opposite, as you understand it. Now, memorize those positive reassessments, and then recite them back to me without looking at them. "Now again. Now again. Now again." "Thanks for the turn-around," he said laughing, and hung up.

Completing the Cycle

In the very natural course of events, having observed the flow of the energies of the moon and other cyclical phenomena, the time comes for a return to the beginning. Now this brings you back to the start of this cycle of renewal and self-development we call Reality Co-creation. However, you are not the same person you were when you began the Journey. You are changed. You are wiser. You are awakening. Thus, you return to the beginning of the cycle, yet you are elevated. You could say that you have come full circle, yet you are in a different and more advanced state of consciousness than when you started your Quest. The metaphor here that may serve you is one of the spiral that moves upward. Yes, you go around in a circle, a cycle of development, but at the beginning of the next cycle, you are higher in frequency, higher in compassion, higher in the capacity to Love others.

Exercise:
Consolidate your Findings

Create Sanctuary Now
Gather your written or otherwise recorded Findings that you have documented over the last four weeks.

Empty The Bag: The positive experiences, emotions, thoughts and so on, that you have stored in The Bag, should be physicalized at this time. In other words, from memory and from your notes reconstruct what you put in The Bag. It is enjoyable to recollect pleasant experiences. This should move very quickly for you and should only take a few minutes. Write down what you remember. Read what you have written and congratulate yourself. Endorse yourself for having created these positive states of consciousness.

Look Inside The Box: Look inside your metaphorical Box and note the transformation of negatives into positives. If there are some negatives that remain, let them stay in The Box for a few more days. Physicalize the negatives that have been transformed into positives by writing them down on a piece of paper or recording them in another medium.

Endorse yourself and be grateful for the positive Findings. Put the remaining negative Findings in The Box for further transformation. Read what you have written and congratulate yourself. Endorse yourself for having created these positive states of consciousness.

Back Engineering Findings: Collect your answers to the end of the chapter Back Engineering questions

Lessons Findings: Assemble your answers to the Lessons learned questions from the end of each chapter.

As you assess your Findings, please note trends, coincidences, anomalies and other remarkable aspects of your data. When you are finished with this exercise...

Exercise:
Share your Findings

Create Sanctuary Now

Collecting data as an anthropologist would, examine your Findings and the notes you have made over the course of your Project. Note interesting observations, experiences, events, people you have met on your Quest. Create a Case Study to present to yourself and others. After you awaken you feel a responsibility to tell others. And so, in your favorite medium - text, image, sound, performance - express what you have discovered in your Project and share your Case Study with others for mutual benefit. This need not be an elaborate enterprise. It may be largely symbolic for you the Practitioner. This gives closure to the Project and allows you to move forward with your Findings to begin again.

What have you learned, Dear Reader? When you can answer that question...

Exercise:
Prepare for the Next Quest

Create Sanctuary Now
The moon is going through its phases, even as we speak...

Between Projects
Last Quarter Moon
Retreat

Epilogue

Retreat

Please observe that here in our interpretation we are ascribing two different meanings to the word retreat, with regards to your moon. In the first sense, the moon <u>does</u> seem to retreat back into itself as it wanes, and in the second sense, it <u>does</u> seem to call for a spiritual retreat, in which the human on a path of awakening, and going with the flow of Natural Time, takes advice from the moon, you might say, and goes within to recollect, to reconsider and to renew.

Now this brings to a close our little treatise on the creation of The Vision. I trust that you have enjoyed the exercises and that you are experiencing perceived success with your Project. Please remember, here, as I have stated in all of my books, in terms of assessing your efforts in these arcane practices, please be gentle, Dear Reader. Yes, please be gentle and Loving with yourself as you assess whether your Vision Statement has been realized. A truly successful Project is one in which the Practitioner learns something about themselves that they did not know previously. This is success, from my perspective. Also, if you have felt, even for just a fraction of a second, the ecstasy that comes from contact with your Higher Centers of Awareness, this too is success. If you have had moments, minutes or hours of successful embodiment of the state of consciousness we call Loving Understanding and Courage, kudos to you. For it is from these small victories that grow what some have called the "classic awakening experience." The white light phenomenon emerges.

Now I sincerely hope that all of you, however you self-assess your efforts in this practice, will try it again, perhaps during the next 28 days of the moon. Then you may see why I was so insistent on your getting to know this moon of yours more deeply and more intimately. This is all there is, my friend. This is All That Is, in fact. I will leave it at that. I trust that you have found what you were looking for...

Ritual of Sanctuary

The Ritual of Sanctuary was presented to readers in our book on **Soul Evolution** when we first began to emphasize direct exploration of the Unknown Reality. We felt that the reader would require some personalized protection in their experimentation.

The most simple form of the Ritual is to imagine, prior to psychic pursuits, a golden Light surrounding you. Nothing harmful can penetrate this field of Light. It has a healing protective influence. You may certainly use this simplified form while you go about creating your own Ritual.

The object here is to generate positive energies with your creative consciousness. Try listing on a piece of paper your positive beliefs and ideas that denote security, peace, and protection. The next step would be, perhaps artistically, to distill these potent concepts down into an image, statement, or physical object that Resonates with the protective energies. Naturally you may include gestures, visualizations, or any other evocative materials.

Practice your Ritual until you can create at-will the state of Sanctuary within your own consciousness. Only you will know when you are successful.

Glossary

Definitions for the concepts Seth discusses in this book.

All That Is - The energy source from which all life sprung throughout the multitude of Universes, transcending all dimensions of consciousness and being part of all. Also referred to as the Logos and Evolutionary Consciousness.

Altared States - Ritualizing and making sacred the mundane activities of existence creates elevated states of consciousness.

Ancient Wisdom - The knowledge of the magicians, shamans, witches and healers of the past.

Appreciation - Profound comprehension with Loving Understanding. A thorough expression of gratitude and humility for what you are experiencing and creating.

Awakening - As the Ancient Wisdom is remembered by humanity, an awareness of the greater reality is experienced by individuals.

Back Engineering - the momentary practice of selecting from the current Reality Creation those elements that represent the Best Case Scenario.

Beliefs - Ideas, images, and emotions within your mental environment that act as filters and norms in the creation of Personal Realities.

Best Case Scenario - The ideal outcome for your Reality Creation Project exists in the Probable Future within the Pre-manifestation Domain.

Bleedthroughs - Momentary experiencing of lives being lived in other timeframes and other systems of reality.

Catharsis - Recovering lost aspects of the Essential Identity.

Co-creation - You co-create your reality with the limitless creative energies of All That Is.

Common Trance - The consciousness of the status quo collective. Supports consumerism and blind obedience to authority.

Consciousness Units (CU's) - The theorized building blocks of realities. Elements of awarized energy that are telepathic and holographic.

Consecutive Positive Assessments (CPA's) - A technique of positive Reality Creation, in which the student finds something positive, something worthwhile in each experience in physical reality.

Courage - Courage and Loving Understanding replace fear and anger in the creation of Positive Realities.

Denial - The ego/intellect prevents the learning of Lessons by denying the truth of the matter.

Dimensions - Points of reference from one reality to the other with different vibrational wavelengths of consciousness.

Divine Day - The student attempts to live a complete waking day while maintaining contact with the Energy Personality.

Divine Will - The will is potentiated through ongoing contact and communication with Beings of Light. Also called Intent.

Ego/Intellect - The aspect of the personality that attempts to maintain the status quo reality.

Ecstasy - The positive emotion experienced in contact with the Divine.

Embodiment - Precepts are lived in the creation of improved realities.

Emotional Body - An Inner Senses representation of your current expression in physical reality.

Energy Personality - A being capable of transferring their thought energy inter-dimensionally to physical beings and sometimes using the physical abilities of those beings for communication.

Entity - Being not presently manifested on the physical plane. Also known as a Spirit.

Essential Identity - A truthful representation of the personality as perceived with the Inner Senses.

Feeling-Tone - Thoughts, images, sounds and assorted sensory data that represent a particular state of consciousness, event, or existence.

Fourth-Dimensional Shift - Consciousness expands as the individual experiences an awareness of all Simultaneous Existences. Also called Unity of Consciousness Awareness.

Frequency - Each human being, each blade of grass, each grain of sand vibrates at a particular frequency.

Gestalts of Consciousness - Assemblages of Consciousness Units into Reality Constructs of all types.

gods - Consciousness personalized and projected outward into reality. A self-created projection of the developing ego. See non-physical beings.

Holographic Insert - Teaching aid of the non-physical beings. Multisensory construct experienced with the Inner Senses.

Higher Centers of Awareness - See Energy Personality, Entity and Objective Observer Perspective.

Home Dimension - Home to your Etheric Body after you make your Transition and in between your lives.

Incarnation - To move oneself into another life experience on the physical plane.

Inner Sense - The Soul's perspective. Both the creator and the perceiver of Personal Realities.

Instant Manifestation - In the New Consciousness, there is the potential to experience no lag time in the creation of realities.

Intellectualization - The aspect of the psyche that attempts to figure things out so that the status quo is maintained.

Intention - See Divine Will.

Issues - Your personality aspects that bring you into conflict with others and create negative emotion.

Lessons - Chosen life experiences of the Soul for further spiritual evolution.

Light Body - The etheric body of refined light.

Love - Love with a capital L is the force behind manifestation in the Third Dimension.

Magical Child - The perspective of the researcher that allows for experiencing and creating the existence through the eyes of of the magical, empowered, pre-socialized identity.

Metaphorical Tool - An empowered visualized construct that the researcher uses to explore the physical and the non-physical worlds.

Moment Point - The current empowered moment of awakening. Exists as a portal to all points past, present and future and all Simultaneous Lives.

Multitasking - To function consciously in both the physical Third Dimension and the metaphysical Fourth, Fifth and Sixth Dimensions.

Mystery Civilizations - Foundational civilizations largely unknown to modern science. Some examples are Atlantis, Lemuria and GA.

Negative Emotion - Habitual creation of negative emotions creates enduring negative realities.

Negative Entities - Negative energies that roam the Universes in pursuit of their own power to dominate.

Negative Persona - Rejected and repressed aspects of the personal identity.

Negative Reality - See Negative Emotion.

New Consciousness - Multi-Dimensional Consciousness is available to those who are exploring the Third Dimension with the help of their non-physical Guides.

Nonphysical Beings - By focusing on All That Is, you help to identify and create your Guides, Helpers, Fairies, Angels and so on.

Objective Observer Perspective - Self-created aspect of consciousness that sees beyond the limitations of the ego/intellect. An intermediary position between the ego and the Soul Self.

Percept - Perception creates reality in the Third Dimension through the Inner Senses.

Personal Reality Field - The radius within your self created world within which you have the most control in the creation of Reality Constructs.

Point of Power - The current empowered Moment Point allows the practitioner to make changes within past, present or future lives.

Precept - Empowered concepts of manifestation. Example: you create your own reality.

Pre-Manifestation Domain - Theorized dimension where all realities exist prior to receiving sufficient energy to emerge into the Third Dimension.

Reality - That which one assumes to be true based on one's thoughts and experiences. Also called Perceived Reality.

Reality Creation - Consciousness creates reality.

Reincarnational Drama - Soul Family drama enacted to teach the participants a Lesson in Value Fulfillment.

Resonance - Within the Telepathic Network, CU's assemble, separate and reassemble according to frequency.

Scientist of Consciousness - The researcher studies the phenomena within the Personal Reality Field by testing hypotheses in experimentation. See Precept.

Seth - An energy personality essence that has appeared within the mental environments of humans throughout the millennia to educate and inspire.

Simultaneous Lives - The multidimensional simultaneous experiences of Souls in incarnation.

Simultaneous Time - Everything that can happen does happen in the current timeless moment of creation.

Soul - The non-physical counterpart to the physical human body, the personality, and the mentality. The spiritual aspect of the human.

Soul Evolution - The conscious learning of Lessons without denial or intellectualization.

Soul Family - The group of humans you incarnate with lifetime after lifetime to learn your Lessons together.

Soul Mates - Loving mates who are awakening together.

Spiritual Hierarchy - Beings of Light who have mastered multidimensional levels of experience throughout the Universes and have moved on to higher service in the evolution of all Souls.

Subconscious Projection - Most of your reality is created subconsciously as you project the contents of your subconscious mind into the Third Dimension.

Subtext - The unspoken truth of a statement that is sensed intuitively. It can come in a burst of intuition, or quite subtly as in a growing understanding.

The Christ - The embodiment of The Christ in your World. Also called World Teacher. First described in Seth Speaks.

The Council - Members of the Spiritual Hierarchy. Highly evolved beings that advise Souls on incarnations for their spiritual evolution.

The New World - The Positive Manifestation

The Vanguard - Advocates for humanity and Mother Earth who incarnate together to lead progressive movements of various kinds.

Third Dimension - The physical plane of Earthly existence.

Trance State - The relaxed, focused state of awareness that allows the Scientist of Consciousness to conduct experiments and collect data.

Trust but Verify - You take on faith the material from your Higher Centers of Awareness and you continually verify to confirm this information.

Uncommon Trance - This altared state honors the integrity and authority of the individual. You are inner-directed and naturally abide by the suggestions of your Higher Centers of Awareness.

Value Fulfillment - Consciousness seeks manifestation of itself into all realities via the fulfillment of all values.

Visionary - Reincarnated magicians, shamans, witches and healers in this current timeframe.

Vision Statement - The Visionary creates an empowered oath or proclamation that will guide their efforts in the Reality Creation Project.

When You Walk Across the Room

Dear Reader, when you walk across the room, you are with each movement forward, re-creating your physical body according to your essential identity out of the Consciousness Units that exist as air in front of you; space, you see. It is not a matter of "bringing" your body across the room, it is more a case of re-creating your body in its totality within this field - within this medium, if you prefer - of holographic units of awarized energy: the Consciousness Units.

Step-by-step, then, your sacred identity - this Soul Self - assembles the physical body of you-the-reader from the CUs "in front of it." The CUs - identified as atoms, or molecules, or CUs of air - are transformed into CUs of blood, flesh, and bone.

Now... in the same precise fashion, the birds as they swoop down to feed, are creating from the CUs of air before them, their bird bodies.

But what of the tree, the mountain, you might ask? As the tree sways in the wind, it re-creates itself out of the CUs of earth and air surrounding it. As the mountain endures the weathering forces of rain and wind, it retains its mountain identity and re-creates itself with minute or catastrophic alterations, according to this weathering over time.

CPSIA information can be obtained
at www.ICGtesting.com
Printed in the USA
BVHW040106290121
598875BV00006B/995